An Islāmic Perspective on Management

'Allamah Sayyid Ja'far
Murtaḍā al-'Āmilī ﷾

AL-BURĀQ

Copyright

ISBN: 978-1-956276-53-4
Printed and published by al-Burāq Publications.
Translated and annotated by al-Burāq Publications. Where needed, context and transliterations were added. Some minor edits were made to the translated Arabic text.

Ordering Information
We offer discounts and promotions for wholesale purchases, non-profit organizations, and other educational institutions. Contact us at the email below for further information.

www.al-Buraq.org
publications@al-Buraq.org

First Edition | June 2024

Dedication

We begin by giving all praise and thanks to God ﷻ for giving us the *tawfiq* to translate this book. He has guided us and without Him, we would not have been guided to the straight path embodied by the Prophet Muḥammad ﷺ and the Ahl al-Bayt ﷻ.

This book is dedicated to all the scholars, martyrs and believers who worked tirelessly to promote the pure Muḥammadan path.

We want to also give our thanks and appreciation to all believers from around the world and acknowledge the team which helped al-Burāq Publications complete this work, spending countless hours to make its publication possible. Please recite Sūrat al-Fātiḥah on behalf of them, their families, and their marḥūmīn.

This book is especially dedicated in honor of ʿAllamah Sayyid Jaʿfar Murtaḍā al-ʿĀmilī ﷺ who made tremendous strides in advancing the cause of Islām. Please remember him in your prayers and may God ﷻ have mercy on him and his loved ones.

'Indeed we belong to God, and to Him do we indeed return'

This book was published in honor of
'Allamah Sayyid Jaʿfar Murtaḍā al-ʿĀmilī 🕸

Born: February 9, 1945
Passed: October 26, 2019

Kindly recite
Sūrat al-Fātiḥah upon his soul

Duʿāʾ al-Ḥujjah

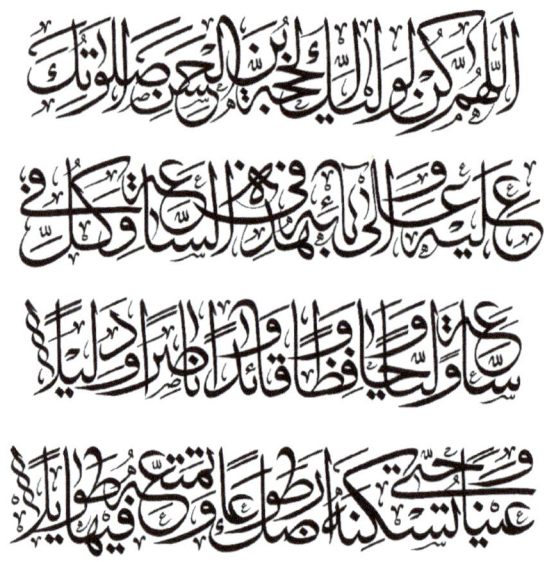

O God, be, for Your representative, the Ḥujjat (proof), son of al-Ḥasan, Your blessings be upon him and his forefathers, in this hour and in every hour: a guardian, a protector, a leader, a helper, a proof, and an eye - until You make him live on the Earth, in obedience (to You), and cause him to live in it for a long time.

Terms of Respect

The following Arabic phrases have been used throughout this book in their respective places to show the reverence which the noble personalities deserve.

ﷻ

Used for God, meaning:
Exalted and Sublime (Perfect) is He

ﷺ

Used for Prophet Muḥammad, meaning:
Blessings from God be upon him and his family

عليه السلام

Used for a man (singular) of a high status, meaning:
Peace be upon him

عليها السلام

Used for a woman (singular) of a high status, meaning:
Peace be upon her

عليهما السلام

Used for men/women (dual) of a high status, meaning:
Peace be upon them both

عليهم السلام

Used for men and/or women (plural) of a high status, meaning:
Peace be upon them all

عجل الله تعالى فرجه الشريف

Used for Imām Muḥammad al-Mahdī, meaning:
May God hasten his return

قدس سره

Used for a deceased scholar, meaning:
May his resting [burial] place remain pure

Transliteration Table

The method of transliteration of Islāmic terminology has been carried out according to the standard transliteration table below.

ء	ʾ	ر	r	ف	f
ا	a	ز	z	ق	q
ب	b	س	s	ك	k
ت	t	ش	sh	ل	l
ث	th	ص	ṣ	م	m
ج	j	ض	ḍ	ن	n
ح	ḥ	ط	ṭ	و	w
خ	kh	ظ	ẓ	ه	h
د	d	ع	ʿ	ي	y
ذ	dh	غ	gh		
Long Vowels					
ا	ā	و	ū	ي	ī
Short Vowels					
‒	a	‒ُ	u	‒ِ	i

Table of Contents

About the Author

Sayyid Jaʿfar Murtaḍā al-ʿĀmilī, son of the late Sayyid Muṣṭafā Murtaḍā al-ʿĀmilī, was born on the 25th of Ṣafar, 1364 (February 9, 1945), in a southern Lebanese town called Dayr Qānūn Rās al-ʿAin, where his father had lived for several years, and then returned to his hometown, ʿAytā az-Zuṭ, which was later changed to the name ʿAytā al-Jabal, Bint Jubayl district, where he settled.

He began religious studies at a young age at the hand of his father, and then went to Najaf, ʿIrāq to pursue his scientific education in 1382 AH (1962 AD).

In Ḥawzah, he studied the introductory and most of the intermediate subjects, and in the year 1388 AH (1968 AD) he decided to move to the religious seminary in the Holy City of Qum, upon the request of his father (may God have mercy on him) and the approval of an *Istikhārat*.

Sayyid Jaʿfar had specialized writings in the field of history and was distinctive in terms of investigation and examination. He participated in *al-Ḥadd* in the field of research and storytelling in order to preserve the ʿAlawīte

Muḥammadan heritage and purify it from impurities.

He recited poetry at a young age, with his father telling him "I want you to be a scholar, not a poet," and then showed him examples of leading scholars who were known for their poetry and forgotten for their religious specificity.

In the Holy City of Qum, he established religious schools, in addition to other various programs.

Sayyid Jaʿfar participated in many scientific conferences in Irān and other countries and contributed to the establishment of the "Arabic School" that is affiliated with the Ḥawzah in the Holy City of Qum.

After 25 years of residence in Qum, he returned to Jabal ʿĀmīl [modern day South Lebanon] in 1414 (1993) and remained in Lebanon for the rest of his life.

Sayyid Jaʿfar established a religious school in Lebanon and named it "the Ḥawzah of Imām ʿAlī b. Abī Ṭālib ﷺ. In addition, he also established the Islāmic Center for Studies.

Sayyid Jaʿfar taught advanced ḥawzah lessons in Bayrūt and he followed his weekly lessons with the interpretation of the Noble Qurʾān and Islāmic and religious culture.

Sayyid Jaʿfar is the author of over 200 books, including biographies of the Holy Prophet ﷺ (35 volumes), Imām ʿAlī ؑ (53 volumes) and Imām al-Ḥusayn ؑ (24 volumes). Even after being diagnosed and treated for cancer, he continued to write.

On Ṣafar 27, 1441 (October 26, 2019) Sayyid Jaʿfar Murtaḍā passed away in a hospital in Bayrūt and was buried in his hometown of ʿAytā al-Jabal.

In short, Sayyid Jaʿfar spent his lifetime in servitude of the religion of Islām. If we were to sum his lifelong work and effort into words, we would not be able to do him justice. He was a historian, a prolific author, and a jurist who defended the truth and preserved the history of Islām. We ask God ﷻ to grant him a lofty rank with the Ahl al-Bayt ؑ and reward him for his unwavering devotion.

Source of Inspiration

In the Name of God, the Beneficent, the Merciful

In Imām 'Alī b. Abī Ṭālib's ﷺ will (after Ibn Muljam (may God curse him) hit the Imām) to Imām al-Ḥasan and Imām al-Ḥusayn ﷺ, Imām 'Alī ﷺ said:

"I command you and all my children and members of my family and whoever my letter reaches to fear God (have taqwā), keep your affairs in order, and maintain good relations among yourselves."[1]

أُوصِيكُمَا وَجَمِيعَ وَلَدِي وَأَهْلِي وَمَنْ بَلَغَه كِتَابِي، بِتَقْوَى الله، وَنَظْمِ أَمْرِكُمْ، وَصَلَاحِ ذَاتِ بَيْنِكُمْ...

---

[1] Sharīf Raḍī, Muḥammad b. al-Ḥusayn, *Nahj al-Balāghah*, Vol. 3, p. 76, Letter 47.

Foreword

In the Name of God, the Beneficent, the Merciful

Praise be to God, Lord of the Worlds, and may his peace and blessings be upon Muḥammad and his pure family, and may His perpetual curse be upon all their enemies until the Day of Judgement.

These are simple words with which I sought to explain the advice of Imām Jaʿfar al-Ṣādiq ﷺ to some of his followers, in which he drew his mode of work with the authorities at the time regarding public affairs and specified for them how to deal with matters they face.

The commandment, albeit short in its structure, is simple and clear in its meaning, yet it is rich in connotations, is eloquent in its phrasing, is wonderful in its indications, is lofty in its descriptions, its effects are beautiful, its goals are great, and its purposes are far-reaching.

As such, I was keen to contribute to drawing these meanings closer to the mind, simplifying its content for those who seek it, and facilitating their access to it, even if only in an amount equivalent to my article and the reality of my situation—based on "my ability dictates the value of my offering."

And from God ﷻ, I derive strength and help and ask for righteousness and guidance in words and deeds, and upon Him, I rely on and through His Prophet ﷺ and the Ahl al-Bayt ﷻ I beseech and beg; indeed, He is the Powerful Guardian.

Friday night, Shawwāl, 14, 1439 AH.

June 29, 2018 AD.

Lubnān (Lebanon), ʿAytā al-Jabal (formerly ʿAytā az-Zuṭ), Jabal ʿĀmil, Bint Jubayl.

ʿAllamah Sayyid Jaʿfar Murtaḍā al-ʿĀmilī

Wonders and Masterpieces in Administrative Affairs

Imām Jaʿfar al-Ṣādiq ﷺ said to some of his followers — when he had gained authority, and it became his responsibility — instructing them to adhere to this advice:

"Know that being occupied with minor aspects disrupts the critical affairs and that, conversely, singling out critical matters comes at the expense of the minor ones, eventually turning them into crucial issues. The ruler acts with these two traits, and his lack of trust [in others in fulfilling assigned tasks] eventually leads him to abandon contentment. So he becomes like a river between many smaller rivers, into which the valleys' torrents flow out; if it tried to carry all the water gushing into it, it would overflow and become submerged, thus diminishing any of its benefits and resulting in harm to it instead. If it were to branch out [some of the water going into smaller streams], the load would lessen, and its waterbanks would come alive and fertile again. So start with the critical, and do not forget to look at the minor matters as well.

Assign someone to compile the small matters and present them to you in two batches or more according to their abundance.

Personally undertake today's work before tomorrow's work piles over it. Otherwise, as mentioned earlier, the river will overflow.

Fill your available time each day with the work you have planned for the previous day.

Assign for your capable (or competent or qualified) personnel[2] each day what they will do the next day. And the following day, discuss with them and review what you arranged for them the day prior. And instruct each one what he must undertake or refrain from undertaking, dismissing the incompetent and keeping the competent.

Accompany a fine deed with a fine complement, for you can only attract the rational [person] with the equivalent benevolence. And direct your benevolence to

---

[2] This is a loose translation as no equivalent of *Kufat* exists in English; the term refers to any people who help you achieve sufficiency in your work, i.e., workers, collaborators, associates, aides, or assistants.

the good-doer, thereby disciplining the wrongdoer, for there is no discipline more profound for the wrongdoer than seeing you reward others while not doing as such to him. If this was especially done based on merit, then the one who deserves it shall improve further [in his good-doing and good work], and the negligent shall veer away from what he is in [from his negligence and wrong-doing].

The qualities of a ruler shall encompass the following:

Consulting the advisors,

Guarding their affairs,

Avoiding the presumption of an investigation into people's missteps, faults, and mistakes,

Stabilize your affairs carefully before making decisions."[3]

---

[3] al-Ḥalwānī, *Nuzhatu al-Naẓir wa Tanbīhu al-Khāṭir*, p. 116

Preamble and Introduction

Over the course of their long history, from the time of the Messenger of God ﷺ and to this present day, the followers [Shīʿa] of Imām ʿAlī and the Ahl al-Bayt ﷺ have always suffered at the hands of those who desire this mortal world and have renounced the Hereafter, and they have always been subject to harm, persecution, and exclusion by tyrants and their accomplices.

Breaking through the wall of hatred and repulsion was one of the most arduous challenges facing the Shīʿa, who were always seeking and attempting to effect any change that could allow them some much-needed respite.

Amid their aspiration to make this breakthrough happen, two influential factors contributed to this achievement: the element of *taqiyyah*[4] and the emergence of an extraordinary skill set in various fields.

This is indicated in this commandment above by Imām Jaʿfar al-Ṣādiq ﷺ.

---

[4] Taqiyyah means precautionary dissimulation or denial of religious belief and practice in the face of persecution.

Ultimately, this is a long discussion, so we shall use this as an introduction to what we want to posit and as a basis for action.

Setting Priorities

The Imām ﷺ began by setting forth a very important rule: whoever wants to delve into the thick of work, facing numerous needs that are widespread across many domains, with the ruler requiring him to fulfill these needs and tasks, must realize that he is unable to address all these all at once.

He must also realize that it is not right for him to enter the field of work chaotically and randomly, for that will only lead to confusion and then failure, incapacity, disappointment, and shock...

Even if he wanted to meet the important needs gradually and calmly within the limits of his capacity and energy, he must refrain from seeking to tackle just about any matter that his eye falls on and his hand reaches. Rather, he must abide by the following:

First, he must set priorities and classify actions according to the necessities and situations imposed upon him regarding life, lawfulness, and faith.

Second, he must set his sights on what is major, critical, and important.

Third, he must not be occupied with minor matters and satisfy himself with them, thus neglecting the important affairs and failing to lend them the necessary concern.

Then, the Imām ﷺ said,

> "...and that, conversely, singling out important matters comes at the expense of the smaller ones, which eventually turns them into critical and major matters..."

This establishes another fundamental rule: To be occupied with minor, unimportant matters in the presence of a major matter is not commendable because it disrupts the important, and to disrupt the important leads to the corruption of affairs. Similarly, focusing all work and effort solely on the big and important matters and neglecting the minor is also not a commendable act, for that eventually turns the minor into a major and critical matter, increasing the responsibility that comes with it and the weight attached to it.

Hence, both these work modes are unacceptable as they ultimately defeat the purpose and waste time, leading to corruption and harming the nation and its people.

Tangible Representation

After the Imām ※ indicated the rule he wanted to guide his followers to, established it, and consolidated it clearly, making it self-evident, he returned to it with an analytical and persuasive approach that relied on comparisons between reality and the applied mental perceptions. He gave a tangible example that could be visualized, reinforcing and affirming the emotional conviction of the rule intended to be enshrined in the core of administrative work.

He drew his tangible example from reality, mentioning that it is not a hypothetical matter; rather, it is a matter that is witnessed generally among the authorities. Any authority or government or ruler usually does not trust other people to accomplish the tasks he assigned to them because they often procrastinate, waste time, neglect their tasks, and rely on others to get them done [pass them onto others], and they do not do things the right way, instead coming up with what is weak, distorted, and incomplete. The authorities' lack of trust in their workers leads them to turn away from entrusting matters to them in many cases...

Consequently, matters take on a different path, and the head and governor remain in front of two choices.

The first choice, which he conveyed to us via an example, can be presented and clarified as follows:

A ruler shoulders many responsibilities, some of which are major and important, while others are minor and ordinary. His workers across the nations also have duties and tasks, both big and small. If we liken this ruler to a river and his workers to smaller streams, then if his workers did not accomplish their duties, these duties and tasks will circle back to the ruler himself, who will have to handle and tackle them and be responsible for them.

If these small streams that flow in their valleys were to gush into the great river, with all their water pouring therein, such that the river alone carries all the water load brought forth, then the water would drown out this great river, diminishing its benefit and instead resulting in harm, and its water will destroy all that which it submerges along the way.

This is the case for the ruler whose aides do not carry out their duties; their duties will be transferred to him, and he will not be able to handle and accomplish them all, nor will he be able to achieve any of his other work. In other words, if he wanted to shoulder the responsibility of all that the smaller streams brought to him and cast over him, then the water load of these small streams would submerge the river—which is the ruler in this case—and his work will thus be tainted with imperfection, deficit, and corruption.

Only if the water carried by the streams were distributed and spread out in various channels and passages, flowing through different bends and folds, would life spring back and goodness ensue.

Through this example, the fundamental rule for the accomplishment of any work becomes clear; in this regard, a worker must abide by the following:

He must begin with the important and should not be preoccupied with minor matters.

It is also not right to focus solely on the important and forget about minor matters, resulting in disruption and corruption.

The second choice entails the main person responsible for handling the major and important matters. As for the minor issues, he must appoint someone (or more) to compile them, and he either assigns the tasks or duties to this appointed person or group of people all at once or over several batches, depending on their abundance.

These two aspects are fundamental to accomplishing work effectively and successfully, and we will observe that the rest of this will focus on these two aspects.

Before we discuss the rest of what the Imām ﷺ mentioned, we first highlight the following:

Compiling and Presenting

The Imām ﷺ said,

> "Assign for the small matters someone to compile them and present them to you in two batches or more according to their abundance."

We benefit from this as follows:

The Imām commanded that one appoint someone to compile the minor matters, and he did not say to appoint someone to handle and accomplish these matters. Perhaps because he is responsible for handling these matters, he cannot pass them on to someone else so that this other person becomes responsible. This is because the ruler first gave him [the person initially put in charge] this responsibility, so if he sought the assistance of someone else, it did not relieve him of the responsibility. Similarly, the public fund [Bayt al-Māl] does not cover any expenses resulting from this transfer of tasks or duties because the remuneration was already paid to the person in charge, and it does not offer payment twice for the same job. So, if the person originally responsible for the matter sought the assistance of someone, it should come at his expense and on his account personally.

Moreover, some of these minor matters might only need a little time to accomplish; for instance, it could be merely making a signature, stamping a transaction, or issuing an order to purchase someone specific. Furthermore, presenting the compiled tasks to the person in charge enables him to identify the qualifications he must look for in the candidates to whom he wishes to assign these tasks.

Another matter that must be highlighted is that the continuous presentation of the tasks [and the progress achieved] to the main responsible person prevents the aides and appointees from having to go beyond their capacity or overstepping their boundaries. This also facilitates accountability or the fulfillment of rights in case of a violation.

His saying, "in two batches or more," indicates that the presentation of minor matters should be conducted on an investigative basis. That is, the abundance of minor issues should not lead the person in charge to be lenient when examining them and determining their nature, for this leniency can encourage others to insert among them what is major and critical.

Prioritizing the Day's Work

Then, he said,

> "Personally undertake the day's work before tomorrow's work accumulates over it, such

that the river mentioned above fills up [and risks overflowing]."

This passage raised the following points:

First, the Imām ﷺ did not say,

"Don't postpone your day's work to tomorrow."

Rather, he commanded his followers to take on the day's work personally and not to assign it to someone else.

Second, someone could be responsible for the day's work that no one else could undertake. Moreover, this could be work that the person doesn't have to do personally, as is the case for financial matters not assigned to him by a spokesman; rather, the person takes it upon himself and chooses to do it.

This is evident in his saying "the day's work," where he did not attribute the work to any specific person.

Third, when the Imām ﷺ said "personally undertake," the aim is not to accomplish the work even if other people did it. Rather, the objective is to achieve the work through the effort of the person originally responsible for it—the person addressed in this will.

Fourth, the accumulation of tomorrow's work over the day's work means that the work is extended and could become double what it originally was. Consequently, he will require more energy than he would've needed to finish the work on the first day. This means that the amount of work and the time needed for it increases in terms of the effort required, becoming double what it originally was. Hence, the river fills up and overflows, diminishing its benefits and resulting in harm. This could only be mitigated if the water was redistributed to other streams so the river's banks could come alive and green again, full of fertile soil and growth.

Pre-Planning

Then, the Imām ﷺ said,

> "Fill your free time every day with the work you have drawn for it yesterday."

This guides us to aspects we need in the fields of work, including the following:

A man should refrain from procrastinating on his day's work such that it becomes connected with tomorrow's work, but he must also plan to finish some work for the following new day in the previous day.

This indicates that planning what must be done must go beyond the day's work and encompass some of the later work meant for the following day.

This means that the person in charge must possess the power of supervision, be able to accurately assess how matters are progressing, and predict what might arise in terms of needs and demands.

It also indicates the responsible person's ability to control and act upon whatever falls into his hands, filling up his future free time immediately when the time comes without having to invest new effort.

Furthermore, this passage can be understood in another way that differs completely from what was discussed above.

Noticeably, the content of the will until this point revolves around "busying oneself" and not about "working".[5]

As is known, "busying oneself" with something differs from "working" on something. Busying oneself is the opposite of idling and doing nothing, and it involves distracting oneself with something from something else.

As for "working," it engages in trade, manufacturing, a specific action, etc. Work includes all actions of the heart and limbs [i.e., intention and application]. It is also said that work is what is done over an extension of time, meaning that they work on something for as long as necessary. However, this contrasts an action, as evident in the verse:

﴿أَلَم تَرَ كَيفَ فَعَلَ رَبُّكَ بِأَصحَابِ الفِيلِ﴾

a-lam tara kayfa faʿala rabbuka bi-ʾaṣḥābi l-fīlī

⟨Have you not regarded how your Lord dealt with the Men of the Elephant?⟩[6]

That is, action can come suddenly and all at once, not over some time.

Moreover, the term work is only applied to what involves thought and deliberation, and that is why it is associated with sciences and knowledge. As such, action is more general than work.[7]

Therefore, busying oneself is mostly related to passing time while doing something, serving as a distraction from something else. Meanwhile, working means accomplishing something via deliberation and thought over a specific period, and it does not serve as a distraction from something else.

The passage in discussion revolves around the concept of "busying oneself" and not work or action, meaning that it aims to establish the following:

---

[6] Sūrat al-Fīl, Verse 1.

[7] See: Shartūnī, Sa'īd al-Khūrī, *Aqrab al-Mawārid fī Faṣḥ al-'Arabīyah wa-al-Shawārid*, ch. *al-'Amal*.

Man must accomplish his day's work and prepare for tomorrow's work, and this is not confined to his thoughts and plans at the present moment. Rather, he must also consider, think, plan, draw, and supervise the mode of work for what comes next after the present moment.

He must dedicate some free time from the previous day, during which he can make something [planning or so] for the benefit of the following day. In this way, the previous day aids and paves the way for the following day, so he is not burdened with worries and distractions when the next day comes upon him. Rather, the preparation done in the previous days provided him with sufficient space and time to undertake the day's work adequately with energy, strength, dominance, and mastery. This is made possible because he has eliminated all burdens and distractions in the previous day and has thus concentrated his focus on accomplishing the requirements of the following day.

Furthermore, his ﷺ words "with the work you drew for it yesterday" indicate that the current day's work must be pre-planned and drawn on the previous day and that the work of every day must be accomplished on that same day, which is evident

in his words "Fill your free time every day with the work you drew for it yesterday."

With this deep and precise instruction, he concluded his talk about the major and important matters and how to tackle them.

Who Specifies the Tasks?

Afterward, he moved on to the second stage: tackling the minor matters by employing the assistance of aides whom he called "workers".[8]

In this regard, the Imām ﷺ said,

> "Assign for your workers every day what they will do tomorrow."

This passage highlights the following:

A helper should not be the one to set the work mode for himself, assigning what he leaves out and what he undertakes during his work shift. Rather, this matter returns to the main person responsible

---

[8] As noted earlier, this is a loose translation as no equivalent of *Kufat* exists in English; the term refers to any people who help you achieve sufficiency in your work, i.e., workers, collaborators, associates, aides, or assistants.

for the task it was first delegated; he must divide it and assign it to his aides.

The person in charge [to whom the overall duty was delegated initially] is responsible and accountable for it, and he will receive a reward or punishment for it; so, it is only natural that he assigns tasks to his workers and helpers.

The Imām ﷺ mentioned that his workers' tasks required the following day must be assigned by him for them on their previous day. This helps them relax mentally and prepares them to undertake what is asked of them. This also prevents them from resorting to excuses such as claiming that they were surprised with the nature of the task, that they are unable to undertake it, that they do not have the necessary means to do so, or that they have been asked to do something beyond their capacity.

Hence, assigning tasks the previous day enables them to voice any objections (if applicable) beforehand. This also gives the responsible person in charge (such as the project manager) the opportunity to adjust his requirements or reassign them to another team able to fulfill his criteria and the purposes underlying the mission.

In this passage, the Imām ﷺ talked about these workers above "working" and not "busying themselves," and so he commanded that the person in charge take it upon himself to make a list of the work required of them in the following day. He ﷺ did say, "Assign for them what they should busy themselves with on the following day." This is according to what we posited earlier about the concept of "busying oneself" lacking the seriousness, strength, and liveliness implied in the term "work." As such, the act of being distracted with something is more implied by the concept of "busying oneself" rather than "working."

Interestingly, most employees these days view their work time as merely passing time, having no value or benefit, and that is why they come up with ways to distract themselves and finish their work as soon as possible, even if it involves forbidden or abhorrent acts.

Discussing and Reviewing the Workers' Tasks

Then, the Imām ﷺ continued,

> "And the following day, discuss with them and review what you arranged for them yesterday."

This passage highlights the following:

Assigning tasks to the aides and workers is only part of the path. Rather, follow-up is necessary by discussing the work he arranged for them on the previous day and inquiring about the overall situation and progress.

This can be done either by reminding them of their tasks at the beginning of the day and then discussing and reviewing what they have achieved thus far at the end of the day, and one can suffice with the second over the first.

The Imām ﷺ specified the time when this inquiry and follow-up should occur. He did not leave it up to the discretion of the lead person in charge or allot it to his free time.

Notice that he specified the time to inquire [about their work] is on the same day their assigned tasks are due. That is, after they finish the work of that day, he meets with them and checks what they have achieved to see if it matches the criteria he specified for them on the day before in terms of the amount of work, the mode or characteristics of work, or the quality...

Notice that he ﷺ did not say, "Discuss what you arranged for them." Rather, he said, "Discuss with them." That highlights how important it is for them to be present there and for him to receive what they have worked on directly from them. As such, this also indicates he should only check on or review their work in their absence or with them, confirming that what is being presented to him is the finished outcome of the work they are responsible for and asked about.

The submission and reception of the assigned work in this way make it incumbent on them to fulfill the demand according to the specifications, quality, and quantity specified because any lack or deviation from these requirements will embarrass them, forcing them to resort to excuses to justify it or attempt to cover it up and obscure any ways that might reveal it. In turn, this carries the risk of their exposure and a fall in their status, and they could even lose their position and job along with that.

Results of the Review

Afterward, the Imām ﷺ said,

> "Communicate to each one an evaluation of his work, deeming it either competent or

incompetent, so dismiss the incompetent and keep competent."

This passage revolves around the review results that he commanded to be done on the same day of their work before they leave the workplace. In this regard, the Imām ﷺ indicated the following:

After the lead person in charge (such as the project manager or head of the department) has reviewed what they have achieved thus far and compared it with what was initially arranged for them, he must face his aides with the honest truth. As such, he must not overlook any negligence, nor should he hide the results of his review and cover up for whoever did not fulfill the demand.

Perhaps the words "communicate to each one an evaluation of his work" means that he should honestly confront each individual with the results of their work and highlight all its specifics in detail.

The Imām ﷺ said "to each one" to indicate that it is not sufficient to make a public announcement that summarizes the overall specifics of the individuals' work and hides their effects, highlighting the results of the majority through general properties and observed trends that do not distinguish the individuals from each other.

The phrase "deeming it either competent or incompetent" is perhaps to indicate that the lead person in charge should not only highlight an error or lack in their work but also remind them of the ensuing negative consequences and indicators of failure, on one hand, or the competence of the individuals and the energy and capacity they demonstrated in undertaking their responsibilities, on the other hand, thus distinguishing between the ones who are unable to fulfill their duties and those who are.

Based on the review results, it is prudent to make firm decisions, leaving no space for laxity and negligence or bias and favoritism.

The decision is then executed by dismissing the incompetent person from the workplace and keeping the competent, able one in his position.

Public Commendation and Praise

Then, the Imām ﷺ proceeded to say,

"Reward a beautiful deed with a beautiful saying, for you can only attract the rational [person] with the equivalent benevolence."

In this passage, he ﷺ indicated the following:

It is not sufficient to keep the competent worker in his position, perhaps because doing so could be interpreted as acting on a whim or resulting from selfishness or a love of preserving interests and attaining certain goals.

Furthermore, the person who was kept in his position may also feel that he achieved what he did through his hard work and effort, with the sweat of his brow and forethought, owing this to no one. Hence, merely keeping him in his position is no sign of doing good by him and being gracious to him; rather, he would feel like the one doing good and being gracious and thus deserving of thanks.

For this reason, it is prudent that the person whose work is praised must feel that there is gratitude for the beauty of his deed and that it has elevated him to a unique status that goes beyond practical and material interests to the convergence of hearts, resulting in feelings of contentment, aspiration, and further affection and harmony. In return, this invites him to reciprocate with the same, and these feelings grow steadily in him, perhaps reaching a point where he really feels that it is your right over him that he considers your interests as his, your money as his, what pleases, pleases him as well, and what is good for as good for him too. Hence, your work with him increases that much in honesty, sincerity, serenity, and purity, and he becomes increasingly worthy of staying and continuing to work with you.

That is why the Imām ﷺ said,

> "Reward a beautiful deed [the workers' and aides' actions] with a beautiful saying."

That is, make them both (the deed and the saying) mutual, harmonious, and alike in their beauty.

What is meant here with "a beautiful saying" is to praise the worker and his actions and commend him, highlighting his virtues, elevating his status, and indicating that his good performance, sound and well-founded thinking, and sincere deliberation distinguished his work from others.

Notice that the Imām ﷺ meant with the word "reward" that his work—although it has ended in benefit to you [the overall responsible person] and has fulfilled a need or demand—remains his own; it is his achievement, it should be attributed to him, and he takes it with him wherever he goes. Thus, highlighting the beauty of his work with an equally beautiful saying is doing good by him... This, in turn, invites him to reciprocate the goodness and kindness with the same, and he thus feels himself bound in converging with you, being in harmony with you, and being sincere to you.

Because an action or deed comes from a person by his own choice, even if all at once—as discussed previously—it could be beautiful or not. Hence, the action or deed must be described with the adjective fitting it, and that is why the Imām ﷺ said here: "a beautiful deed."

Notice that the Imām ﷺ said,

> "...for you can only attract the rational [person] with the equivalent benevolence."

This indicates that if something wrong, harmful, and destructive were disguised in a deceptively positive and nice image, the ignorant would set out towards it without reflection or contemplation, thus falling into harm and danger.

That is the case for the small-minded, such as children and foolish people who are also allured by shapes, sizes, and colors and spend their time and effort on them without any benefit or return.

As for the rational person, in benevolence, he looks for the purity of the soul, the beauty and sincerity of intentions, the purity of the heart, and the innocence of the soul. Then, feelings converge and mix, and the souls entwine together in an embrace. Ultimately, the rational person realizes this benevolence is the purest and most lasting element in relationships.

Benevolence to the Good-Doer is Punishment for the Wrongdoer

The Imām ﷺ then said,

> "And be benevolent to the good-doer, thereby punishing the wrongdoer, for there is no punishment more articulate for the wrongdoer than seeing you do good to others while not doing good to him, especially if that was from you due to merit; in this way, the one who deserves it improves further [in his good-doing and good work], and the negligent moves away

from what he is in [from his negligence and wrong-doing]."

This passage presents a reformative approach in the field of penalties for administrative violations as follows:

Penalties for administrative violations could include imprisonment, financial fines, withholding some allowances or benefits, or dismissal from work. However, none of these penalties involve commending those who did well and were good while neglecting the ones who did wrong, fell short, and did not achieve the desired outcomes.

Counting this among the various penalties does not mean merely considering the negative effects on the person's feelings and psychological state and the like. Rather, a positive education element is included in this sort of punishment: commending the good-doer and appreciating his character, praising his good performance, and highlighting his practical innovations and the masterpieces of his workmanship, all directly impacting his determination to continue his success. This becomes one of the reasons for sharpening his motivation to achieve greater and better results.

This is what the Imām ﷺ indicated when he said,

> "…the one who deserves it improves further [in his good-doing and good work]…"

Furthermore, this also introduces the wrongdoer into a cycle of remorse and regret for his negligence, disappointment, and the bitterness of being forbidden this show of appreciation. This also makes him taste the humiliation of failure, especially when he receives those condescending and perhaps scornful glances. Indeed, such moments are very hard to bear; how bitter it must feel for the one who brings this unnecessarily upon himself.

The Imām ﷺ said,

> "…for there is no punishment worse for the wrongdoer than seeing you do good to others while not doing good to him…"

This can mean benevolence in action [the wrongdoer can see it], and this is about what he ﷺ posited, "And be benevolent to the good-doer, thereby punishing the wrongdoer." Moreover, his saying, "Reward a beautiful deed with a beautiful saying," refers to another type of benevolence: verbal benevolence and practical benevolence.

His ﷺ saying, "...for there is no punishment more articulate for the wrongdoer than seeing you do good to others," makes us wonder why he chose the word "more articulate" and not "more severe." In this regard, the goal behind the punishment here is not the unconstrained infliction of punishment and hurting the wrongdoer, even if it were to gloat over the person who subjected you to harm, loss, or lack. Rather, the objective of the punishment is to convey and articulate a reformative message to the wrongdoer, which makes him contemplate and rethink until he reaches new convictions. Such a transformation in his thoughts could include the mere feeling that the good-doer was not rewarded on a whim, nor did the good-doer perform a miracle that no one else can; rather, the reason is very simple and easy. Everyone can do what the good-doer accomplished and even more, and they can earn the same (or more) praise, commendment, and benevolence that he did. This is what the Imām ﷺ highlighted when he said, "... and the negligent moves away from what he is in [from his negligence and wrong-doing]."

We also notice that the Imām ﷺ said,

> "...more articulate for the wrongdoer than seeing you do good to others..."

He did not say, "more articulate for the wrongdoer than you doing good to others," even though this phrase is briefer than the first. So why did he mention seeing or witnessing benevolence and not the benevolence in itself?

Our answer is that he ﷺ wanted to communicate to that man the most articulate and influential images, one in which mental perception meets the sensory images. Here, it is noteworthy that what is perceived by the senses differs and varies in its strength to influence the formation of mental convictions related to these perceptions. What the ear hears could be the truth, but it could also be false or distorted. Similarly, what you touch with your hand could be mixed up with many other things; for instance, the liquid might be water, and it might not be water as well. A solid might be a rock, but it might also be wood.

As such, all things that can be perceived via the senses carry different possibilities. However, what a person sees with his eyes can only be the truth distinct from all other visible things; thus, its contribution to forming mental convictions is the highest and most intense.

The Imām ﷺ said,

> "...especially if that was from you due to merit..."

Here, he is saying that the negligent, if he sees your benevolence to the good-doer, will realize that this benevolence, kindness, flattery, and praise did not come in vain nor on a whim. Rather, there is reason and motive behind them, and this reason is nothing but the mastery of his work and his fulfillment of what was asked of him in the best way. When the negligent sees this benevolence and realizes the reason for which this person is being elevated and praised, he will return to himself and wake up from his negligence, realizing that he could have earned that which the good-doer has earned because the reason behind it is realistic and possible, and achieving it is easy. In turn, this exacerbates the negligent person's remorse and grief.

Consulting the Advisors

Then, the Imām 🕮 said,

> "The strength and authority of the ruler stem from [...] consulting the advisors."

Here, we note the following:

This statement from the Imām 🕮 establishes a rule that applies to the ruler as he sits at the helm of all authorities. It is also valid for every responsible person (for example, the manager, head, or leader.) in his dealings with his aides and all others whom he has a connection with in their fields of work.

This rule is based on four elements that the ruler needs in his successful administration and that lends him trust and confidence in the stability of affairs and the strength and firmness of the system. These elements are the following:

Consulting the advisors,

Guarding their affairs

Abandoning the questioning and investigation into people's missteps and sins

Deliberating matters carefully (examining them and consulting others before making decisions)

Concerning consulting advisors, we highlight the following:

First, this ensures the ruler is outside the circle of tyranny by opinion.

Second, this distances the ruler from feeling self-centered in that it gives him a sense of need for others and a goal outside his limits.

Third, he feels that his authority does not entitle him to act according to his whims, free from all restrictions and transgressing all limits. Instead, he acknowledges that there are constraints he must observe and restrictions and limits he must not cross.

Fourth, this also makes him feel that he can find what he needs in others, and he thus thinks that it is prudent to get to know the elite among them, weave an intimate relationship with them, make them believe that he trusts them, and rely on them.

Guarding their Affairs

The second basis of orderliness in the authorities' affairs is guarding the advisors' affairs. In this regard, the advisors are the most important pillar in the uprightness of the ruler's command and strength and the preservation and continuity of his rule. Hence, it is prudent that he get to know these advisors and give them the ability and courage to reveal what is kept secret in their minds and what troubles their hearts. This is achieved when they feel safe and secure around him and protected by him, knowing that he does not forsake them and that he defends them, prevents others from doubting them, and protects them from attempts to smear their reputations and dignities. That is because if any of these elements are breached and troubled in such a way that it leads to a disturbance to their stature and dignity, it will cause them great and critical embarrassment. In turn, this may lead them to refrain from elaborating on and talking at great length about the merits and grounds of their advice, rather finding themselves forced to mumble shortly about these, preferring not to fulfill the necessary criteria and elements surrounding their advice. Perhaps they even find themselves forced to conceal what is good, right, and righteous from their advice.

Ultimately, preserving and maintaining the advisors and warding off their bad and harmful qualities is also a means of preserving the ruler and maintaining his rule.

On another note, the Imām ﷺ did not say "guarding the advisors." Rather, he said, "guarding the affairs of the advisors" because what is required is guarding their affairs and status, not their persons. Status and position are the highest and most valuable aspects for a rational person, for there is no value to a man's life if he loses his dignity, reputation, status, and respect. His life and death become no different than the life and death of any other creature, even non-human creatures.

Abandoning Questioning

The third element that the Imām ﷺ mentioned is abandoning the questioning and investigation into people's missteps, faults, and mistakes, among the important things that ensure the uprightness of matters and the stability and continuity of his rule. That is because of the following:

Certainly, Islām established the foundation of enjoining good and forbidding evil and made it the collective obligation of the entire nation on the level of each individual, as God ﷻ said:

﴿كُنتُمْ خَيْرَ أُمَّةٍ أُخْرِجَتْ لِلنَّاسِ تَأْمُرُونَ بِالْمَعْرُوفِ وَتَنْهَوْنَ عَنِ الْمُنكَرِ وَتُؤْمِنُونَ بِاللَّهِ﴾

﴿kuntum khayra 'ummatin 'ukhrijat li-n-nāsi ta'murūna bi-l-ma'rūfi wa-tanhawna 'ani l-munkari wa-tu'minūna bi-l-llāhi﴾

﴿You are the best nation [ever] brought forth for mankind: you bid what is right and forbid what is wrong, and have faith in God﴾[9]

However, at the same time, God ﷻ prohibited spreading the immorality committed and circulating its mention. Rather, He has forbidden the person who has committed a violation from revealing it, and He even preferred that the one who wishes to purify himself with the legal punishment to cover himself [hide his sin] and resort instead to the door of repentance and regret, sincerely seeking forgiveness.

---

[9] Sūrat Āl 'Imrān, Verse 110.

God  said:

﴿يَا أَيُّهَا الَّذِينَ آمَنُوا توبوا إِلَى اللَّهِ تَوْبَةً نَصُوحًا﴾

﴿yā-'ayyuhā lladhīna 'āmanū tūbū 'ilā llāhi tawbatan naṣūḥan﴾

﴿O you who have faith! Repent to God with sincere repentance!﴾[10]

That is, one must be sincere in honesty and sincerity and sincere in terms of being steadfast in it [the repentance], ensuring perseverance and continuity.

It is well known that if the ruler sought to closely track the people's mistakes and missteps, he would embarrass them and drive them beyond their limits. In turn, this increases their feelings of alienation and anger as the one who is subjecting them to this humiliation is the same person with whom they expect to find protection, aid, and compassion. They even see him as a merciful father [initially], but if he were to scrutinize and search for their flaws and failures, their animosity for him would grow far greater than their animosity for

---

[10] Sūrat al-Taḥrīm, Verse 8.

anyone else. That is because the ruler possesses a power they cannot confront, and because of such a policy, the ruler proves to be an element of disappointment and failure and a source of fear and terror.

Therefore, it is prudent that the ruler abandons such behavior of questioning and investigation into flaws and sins of people, as the Imām ※ said.

Careful Deliberation of Matters

Finally, one of the deficiencies in governance and rulers is that they need to observe the rules of legitimacy, reason, and rationality when deliberating matters they encounter. They do not appoint - for the people - competent judges who judge them according to correct measures and without leniency, immoderateness, or negligence.

Furthermore, among the rulers are those who hasten the persecution of people based on a mere rumor, an illusion that occurred to the ruler's mind, or unreliable news, thus violating the sanctities of the people.

Thus, the Imām ※ commanded the careful deliberation of matters, that is, to ask for evidence and proof for a matter, for [otherwise] it is not permissible to seize people based on an accusation. That is because accusations, illusions, rumors, or news come from someone who cannot be trusted; if all such matters and the like were to manage and affect the country and its people, then the people would be left without a sense of security. Their pain and bitterness would grow even worse if the source of their fear were the same person [the ruler] whom they hoped to be their source of safety, goodness, mercy, and compassion.

Main Points and Results

We conclude from all those above the following:

The necessity of pre-planning for any work

Refraining from entering any work in a random and chaotic manner

Determining priorities and classifying work according to necessities

Distinguishing major business from minor business

Starting with major and important matters and not being preoccupied with minor matters

Preoccupation with the most important affairs should not lead to neglecting other [less] important issues.

The lead responsible person in charge takes care of the most important affairs personally.

Appointing someone to compile the minor matters and manage them and then present them to him in one batch or more, according to their abundance

The necessity to investigate all minor matters and their details, no matter how many

Workers and Aides

Competent workers and aides should be appointed to carry out the work.

The lead person should be the one to assign tasks to his workers.

Tasks for the workers should be assigned every day for the next day.

The workers must be informed on the previous day about what is required of them on the following day.

The lead person in charge is responsible and accountable for the complete and sound achievement of work, and he is the one who is rewarded or punished.

The lead responsible person should check on and review the work progress of his aides to confirm that they are working according to the requirements.

This review should be done before the workers leave the workplace.

This review should be done via direct inspection from the person in charge.

This review should be comprehensive and precise.

The work of each worker should be reviewed in the presence of each worker himself.

The person in charge should inform the workers of areas that need to be corrected.

Based on the review results, responsible people should make appropriate and firm decisions without leniency or bias.

The responsible person in charge must demonstrate to each worker how his decisions conform to the work he reviewed.

His decisions must include dismissing the incompetent and keeping the competent (and this decision does not include the competent who made a mistake).

By adopting the principle of material reward for the good-doers, it is understood from the words of the Imām ﷺ that you can only attract the rational person with equivalent benevolence.

Publicly commending, praising, and elevating the status of the good-doer

This praise and commendation and the like should occur in the presence of the negligent or the wrongdoer.

Specifying the reason why the good-doer earned this commendation, displaying his good performance and the mastery of his workmanship, and not sufficing with loose and vague expressions

The wrongdoer's punishment is seeing the benevolence, praise, commendation, and glorification that the good-doer earned, which means avoiding other forms of penalty such as salary cuts, demotion, withholding parts of allowance and benefits, and so on.

The lead person in charge should not impose his opinion and consider it irrevocable.

He has to take advisors,

His advisors must advise him on resolving matters, achieving desired goals, and achieving the required achievements.

He has to establish a mechanism to discover the competent advisor and check whether it is safe to take advantage of.

The lead person in charge must protect his advisors, defend them, prevent them from being doubted and questioned, and prevent their reputations from being smeared, even if legal procedures were to be implemented to achieve this goal.

The lead person should not track the missteps and mistakes of people, including his aides and those who follow his orders.

The lead person should not investigate the secrets of the people and employees with him, which burdens their chests and leads them to engage in excessive concealment in various matters.

The lead person does not have the right to proceed with an order or make a hasty and random decision based on a rumor or thought for which he does not have conclusive evidence. Rather, research and investigation are necessary to ensure the soundness and correctness of the decision and its conformity with the reality of the situation.

Final Word

After this quick and brief presentation of what we understood from this blessed commandment, we can only apologize to the honorable reader for any shortcomings he may have noticed in our understanding of the meaning intended by all or some of its paragraphs. We do not claim to be infallible or encompass everything.

We ask God to reconcile us with what is right and good and to guide us to the path of righteousness; indeed, He is the Powerful Guardian.

Praise be to God, and peace and blessings be upon Muḥammad and his pure family.

Shawwāl 16, 1439 AH

July 1, 2018 AD

ʿAllamah Sayyid Jaʿfar Murtaḍā al-ʿĀmilī